KSE Academy®
c/ Arabial 4, local 2, bajo
Granada 18004, Spain

First published in July 2020

ISBN: 9798663149655

Manufactured on demand by Kindle Direct Publishing.

For further information and resources,
please visit: www.kseacademy.com

Disclaimer
Cambridge C1 Advanced and CAE are brands belonging to The University of Cambridge and
are not associated with KSE Academy or the author of this work.

Use of English Part 4
for C1 Advanced

100 Key Word
Transformation Sentences

Luis Porras Wadley

www.kseacademy.com

Table of Contents

Test 1

For questions **1-6**, complete the second sentence so that it has a similar meaning to the first sentence, using the word given. **Do not change the word given.** You must use between **three** and **six** words, including the word given. Here is an example (**0**).

Example:

0 Making lunch for 8 people requires a lot of work.

DEAL

A ***great deal of work is*** required to make lunch for 8 people.

1 Joe denied having stolen the money from the safe.

NOT

Joe said that _____ the money from the safe.

2 Lucy says that she prefers to listen to music without her headphones.

RATHER

Lucy says that _____ to music with her headphones.

3 Benjamin apologised for being so distracted lately.

CLOUDS

Benjamin apologised _____ lately.

4   I was finally able to study enough, and in the end I even played some video games.

MANAGE

Not only _____ study enough, but also I played some video games in the end.

5   We went hiking over the weekend despite the bad weather.

THOUGH

We went hiking over the weekend _____ bad.

6   Some people still believe that Elvis Presley is well and living on an island.

BE

Elvis Presley _____ well and living on an island.

Test 2

For questions **7-12**, complete the second sentence so that it has a similar meaning to the first sentence, using the word given. **Do not change the word given**. You must use between **three** and **six** words, including the word given. Here is an example (**0**).

Example:

0 My son's best friend drove us to the airport.

LIFT

We **_were given a lift_** to the airport by my son's best friend.

7 Sugary drinks are extremely bad for people's health.

HARMFUL

Sugary drinks _____ people's health.

8 Government measures will cause a change in the way retailers run their business.

ABOUT

Government measures will _____ in the way retailers run their business.

9 The way John talks to his employees will make them rebel against him eventually.

RESULT

The way John talks to his employees _____ rebelling against him eventually.

10   After leaving the restaurant, they all felt as if the waiter had overcharged them unfairly.

OFF

After leaving the restaurant, they all felt they _____ .

11   Marie said that she was very sorry that she had made such a silly mistake.

FOR

Marie _____ made such a silly mistake.

12   Only time would tell if they had made the right choice or not.

OR

Only time would tell _____ chosen correctly.

Test 3

For questions **13-18**, complete the second sentence so that it has a similar meaning to the first sentence, using the word given. **Do not change the word given**. You must use between **three** and **six** words, including the word given. Here is an example (**0**).

Example:

0   My son's best friend drove us to the airport.

LIFT

We **_were given a lift_** to the airport by my son's best friend.

13   Despite not being right, he decided not to tell anyone.

IN

Although he _____ he decided not to tell anyone.

14   Carl refused to tolerate his girlfriend being jealous any more.

PUT

Carl said that he would _____ his girlfriend being jealous any more.

15   Rose was very surprised by her sister's unexpected visit.

BY

Rose's sister unexpected _____ surprise.

16 Thomas will eventually decide to leave his parents' home.

TIME

It's only a _____ the decision of leaving his parents' house.

17 There seems to be seamless integration of all the stories in the film.

PRESENTED

All the stories in the film _____ integrated manner.

18 This new type of plastic is not as bad for the environment as most other types.

FRIENDLY

This new type of plastic is _____ than most other types.

Test 4

For questions **19-24**, complete the second sentence so that it has a similar meaning to the first sentence, using the word given. **Do not change the word given**. You must use between **three** and **six** words, including the word given. Here is an example (**0**).

Example:

0   My son's best friend drove us to the airport.

  LIFT

  We **_were given a lift_** to the airport by my son's best friend.

19   If you come to the party tonight, I promise I'll help you study for your exam over the weekend.

  AS

  I promise to help you study for your exam over the weekend
  _____ to the party tonight.

20   Long-term stress can most certainly affect people's health in a negative way.

  TOLL

  Long-term stress can most certainly _____ people's health.

21   You should have thought twice before bringing that pullover. It's too hot for it.

  NEED

  It's too hot for that pullover. You _____ brought it.

22 He could not conceal his excitement.

UNABLE

He _____ excited he was.

23 People usually have no idea how to write a book.

KNOW

People rarely _____ are written.

24 Most people would be embarrassed to have done what she did.

OF

Most people _____ doing what she did.

Test 5

For questions **25-30**, complete the second sentence so that it has a similar meaning to the first sentence, using the word given. **Do not change the word given.** You must use between **three** and **six** words, including the word given. Here is an example (**0**).

Example:

0   My son's best friend drove us to the airport.

     LIFT

     We _**were given a lift**_ to the airport by my son's best friend.

25   They are right to have a high opinion of John's wife.

     THINKING

     They are not _____ John's wife.

26   Smokers are especially in danger of developing lung cancer.

     RISK

     Smokers are especially _____ from lung cancer.

27   While the bus roared across the plains, she managed for a moment to see the ocean in the distance.

     GLIMPSE

     While the bus roared across the plains, she _____ the ocean in the distance.

28   Tom had no idea that his parents were planning on moving houses.

DARK

Tom's parents had _____ as regards their plan to move houses.

29   The meeting had not gone as planned, but the results were quite satisfactory.

THOUGH

The results were quite satisfactory _____ been different to what was expected.

30   If he made the right decision or not, we will eventually find out.

TIME

Only _____ not he made the right decision.

Test 6

For questions **31-36**, complete the second sentence so that it has a similar meaning to the first sentence, using the word given. **Do not change the word given**. You must use between **three** and **six** words, including the word given. Here is an example (**0**).

Example:

0 My son's best friend drove us to the airport.

   LIFT

   We ***were given a lift*** to the airport by my son's best friend.

31 They finally decided to postpone the match due to heavy rain.

   OFF

   The match _____ due to heavy rain.

32 It was impossible for him to hide how angry he was with his wife.

   HIS

   He found _____ towards his wife.

33 Robert always says that he could not live if he didn't have his smartphone.

   DO

   Robert always says that we would not _____ his smartphone.

34   By the end of the month, we're always struggling with money.

ENDS

We're always struggling _____ by the end of the month.

35   I wouldn't be so upset if you had told me about the party sooner.

PARTY

I wouldn't be so upset if you had let _____ advance.

36   The bad news didn't seem to have any impact on Jack's attitude towards life.

EFFECT

The news seemed to _____ Jack lived his life.

Test 7

For questions **37-42**, complete the second sentence so that it has a similar meaning to the first sentence, using the word given. **Do not change the word given.** You must use between **three** and **six** words, including the word given. Here is an example (**0**).

Example:

0   My son's best friend drove us to the airport.

LIFT

We ***were given a lift*** to the airport by my son's best friend.

37   We had to follow all legal regulations when we set up our real estate enterprise.

ACCORDANCE

We had to set up our real state enterprise _____ legal regulations.

38   I want people to know exactly what happened.

RECORD

I want to _____ about what happened.

39   I only started liking handball when I was in highschool.

TOOK

I only _____ when I was in highschool.

40 Rory said he was feeling a little ill and didn't want to go out.

UNDER

Rory was feeling _____ and didn't want to go out.

41 I'm sure that they have missed the train.

FAILED

They _____ catch the train.

42 We must agree on two colours we don't like, at least.

RULE

We must _____ two colours we don't like.

Test 8

For questions **43-48**, complete the second sentence so that it has a similar meaning to the first sentence, using the word given. **Do not change the word given**. You must use between **three** and **six** words, including the word given. Here is an example (**0**).

Example:

0   My son's best friend drove us to the airport.

   LIFT

   We **_were given a lift_** to the airport by my son's best friend.

43   Tim is the person I was talking to the other day when you saw me.

   TO

   Tim _____ I was talking when you saw me the other day.

44   The weather wasn't good enough so they cancelled the match.

   CALLED

   The match _____ because the weather wasn't good enough.

45   It's not worth trying to convince him, he's determined.

   POINT

   There _____ to convince him, he's determined.

46   Joanne is proud of her son's achievements.

PRIDE

Joanne _____ her son's achievements.

47   I don't feel like going to the cinema tonight.

MOOD

I _____ to go to the cinema tonight.

48   I never meant to give the impression I was a shy person.

ACROSS

I never intended _____ a shy person.

Test 9

For questions **49-54**, complete the second sentence so that it has a similar meaning to the first sentence, using the word given. **Do not change the word given**. You must use between **three** and **six** words, including the word given. Here is an example (**0**).

Example:

0   My son's best friend drove us to the airport.

LIFT

We **_were given a lift_** to the airport by my son's best friend.

49   In the end, I concluded I should do it by myself.

CAME

In the end, _____ I should do it by myself.

50   I have never met anyone as stubborn as your brother.

ACROSS

Never _____ anyone as stubborn as your brother.

51   This issue has to be solved today.

FIND

Measures must be _____ this issue by the end of the day.

52 Citizens are worried about the future of the country.

EXPRESSING

Citizens _____ regard to the future of the country.

53 If you have a student card, you don't have to pay to take the bus.

CHARGE

You can travel _____ if you have a student card.

54 "Thank you very much for all the information you sent me," Joanne told me.

EXTREMELY

Joanne _____ the information I had sent her.

Test 10

For questions **55-60**, complete the second sentence so that it has a similar meaning to the first sentence, using the word given. **Do not change the word given**. You must use between **three** and **six** words, including the word given. Here is an example (**0**).

Example:

0   My son's best friend drove us to the airport.

        LIFT

        We ***were given a lift*** to the airport by my son's best friend.

55   I think you'll have difficulty in coping with his disruptive behaviour.

        EASY

        I think you will _____ up with his disruptive behaviour.

56   When do you think they'll fix the toilets on this floor?

        OUT

        When do you think the toilets will stop _____?

57   I was not surprised to find out that he had been fired.

        CAME

        The fact that he had been fired _____ to me.

58   I actually have a lot less money than what I had at the beginning of the year.

NEARLY

I don't have _____ I had at the beginning of the year.

59   Jenny's house was demolished after she died.

PULLED

Jenny's house _____ away.

60   I am really disappointed with my marks this term compared to the ones last term.

COMPARISON

My marks this term are _____ the ones last term.

Test 11

For questions **61-66**, complete the second sentence so that it has a similar meaning to the first sentence, using the word given. **Do not change the word given**. You must use between **three** and **six** words, including the word given. Here is an example (**0**).

Example:

0   My son's best friend drove us to the airport.

     LIFT

     We _**were given a lift**_ to the airport by my son's best friend.

61   She got the job even though she didn't have any experience in business administration.

     NO

     Despite _____ business administration, she got the job.

62   I will certainly not endanger my life for such a silly sport.

     WILLING

     I am not _____ risk for such a silly sport.

63   "You should never trust strangers, Oliver." said his mother.

     ADVISED

     Oliver's mother _____ trusting strangers.

64   Action films are of no interest to me at all.

APPEAL

Action films _____ the least.

65   In order to dispose of the body, they had to make use of very corrosive chemicals.

GET

Extremely corrosive chemicals were used so _____ of the body.

66   You cannot marry unless you are 18 or over.

LAW

It's _____ married unless you are 18 or over.

Test 12

For questions **67-72**, complete the second sentence so that it has a similar meaning to the first sentence, using the word given. **Do not change the word given.** You must use between **three** and **six** words, including the word given. Here is an example (**0**).

Example:

0   My son's best friend drove us to the airport.

     LIFT

     We ***were given a lift*** to the airport by my son's best friend.

67   My friends think that volleyball is an easy sport to play.

     FIND

     My friends do _____ volleyball.

68   People don't have very positive attitudes towards politicians.

     HIGHLY

     People _____ politicians.

69   We get more confused as we try to find out more about what happened.

     MORE

     The more we try to find out _____ we get.

70 It is advisable not to go swimming immediately after having a copious meal.

AVOID

You ought _____ a swim immediately after having a copious meal.

71 "I am really tired of my job, so I'd like to quit." said John.

UP

John said he would like to quit his job because he _____ it.

72 Liam loves to talk and flirt with women at clubs.

UP

Liam loves to _____ at clubs.

Test 13

For questions **73-78**, complete the second sentence so that it has a similar meaning to the first sentence, using the word given. **Do not change the word given**. You must use between **three** and **six** words, including the word given. Here is an example (**0**).

Example:

0   My son's best friend drove us to the airport.

      LIFT

      We ***were given a lift*** to the airport by my son's best friend.

73   I am really not interested at all in what you are saying.

      SLIGHTEST

      I really don't _____ what you are saying.

74   You don't need to worry about the exam as long as you study hard.

      NO

      If you study hard, there _____ you to worry about the exam.

75   Make sure you call me as soon as you arrive at the airport.

      UPON

      Make sure you give _____ at the airport.

76   I do not intend to marry her any time soon.

NO

I have _____ married to her any time soon.

77   I believe you'll be in trouble if you don't tell your boss.

WATER

I believe you'll be _____ you tell your boss.

78   I am sure you will successfully convince the rest of your team.

BOUND

You _____ convincing the rest of your team.

Test 14

For questions **79-84**, complete the second sentence so that it has a similar meaning to the first sentence, using the word given. **Do not change the word given**. You must use between **three** and **six** words, including the word given. Here is an example (**0**).

Example:

0   My son's best friend drove us to the airport.

    LIFT

    We ***were given a lift*** to the airport by my son's best friend.

79   I believe it's impossible for John to have stolen your computer; he was with me all day.

    BEEN

    It _____ who stole your computer; he was with me all day.

80   It's really not likely that he will be recovering any time soon.

    LIKELIHOOD

    There is very _____ recovering any time soon.

81   "It wasn't me who laughed at Jamie," said Liam.

    FUN

    Liam denied _____ Jaime.

82   I don't have any friends in London, so there's nobody I can stay with.

PUT

My friends _____ because none of them lives in London.

83   "I will stop smoking as soon as I recover from this cold," promised Mark.

CARRY

Mark promised _____ after recovering from that cold.

84   We need to start studying hard soon if we want to pass our finals.

HITTING

We need to start _____ if we want to pass our finals.

Test 15

For questions **85-90**, complete the second sentence so that it has a similar meaning to the first sentence, using the word given. **Do not change the word given**. You must use between **three** and **six** words, including the word given. Here is an example (**0**).

Example:

0   My son's best friend drove us to the airport.

       LIFT

       We _**were given a lift**_ to the airport by my son's best friend.

85   Next time I get a job I expect it to be less challenging than this one.

       CHALLENGES

       I hope _____ than this one.

86   Unfortunately, the fundraiser was quite unsuccessful.

       SUCCESSFUL

       Unfortunately, we weren't _____ funds.

87   You're the most stubborn person I've ever met.

       ANYONE

       Never _____ stubborn as you.

88   As a result of the bad weather, all the crops were ruined.

RESULTED

The bad weather _____ ruined.

89   He is so shy that he doesn't look people in the eye.

CONTACT

He's so shy that he normally avoids _____ people.

90   I made sure that the party was under control at all times.

HAND

I made sure that the party _____ at any time.

Test 16

For questions **91-96**, complete the second sentence so that it has a similar meaning to the first sentence, using the word given. **Do not change the word given.** You must use between **three** and **six** words, including the word given. Here is an example (**0**).

Example:

0 My son's best friend drove us to the airport.

LIFT

We **_were given a lift_** to the airport by my son's best friend.

91 "I wish we had brought the map with us," said Jane.

REGRETTED

Jane _____ map with them.

92 "I hate not having enough money to buy a new house," said Joe.

AFFORD

Joe complained about _____ a new house.

93 I really don't mind which one to take with us.

MAKE

It doesn't _____ which one we take.

94   Jeff spent the whole night playing video games.

LONG

Jeff played video games _____.

95   I like Italian food much better than Indian.

KEENER

I am a _____ food than Indian.

96   If you hadn't had an antidote with you, I would have died for sure.

CARRYING

Had _____, I would have died for sure.

Bonus Sentences

For questions **97-100**, complete the second sentence so that it has a similar meaning to the first sentence, using the word given. **Do not change the word given.** You must use between **three** and **six** words, including the word given.

97   Employees are the highest priority in this company.

     MATTERS

     Employees _____ this company.

98   Did you know that Marcus had informed his boss that he's resigning?

     NOTICE

     Did you know that Marcus had _____?

99   Did you know that he doesn't intend to visit us in the summer?

     AWARE

     Were you _____ of visiting us in the summer?

100   This beer is actually better than I expected.

     EXPECTED

     I had _____ so good.

How to mark and score Use of English Part 4

- Every item (or sentence) weighs 2 points.

- Each test (6 sentences) weighs 12 points.

- Every answer is divided into 2 parts by "|".

- Each half, before and after "|", counts 1 point.

- If you get one half right, you get 1 point. If you get two halves right, you get 2 points.

- To consider that you have been successful in each test (6 sentences), you need at least 8 points.

- When you see "/" it" means that there are two options. This might apply to one or two words in the answer, or to two different answers altogether.

Questions? Comments? Feedback?

Email me at luis@kseacademy.com

And don't forget to keep smiling! :-)

Key

1 he had not | stolen

2 she would rather not | listen

3 for having his head | in the clouds /
for being | in the clouds

4 did I | manage to

5 even though | the weather was

6 is still believed | to be

7 are extremely harmful | to /
have an extremely harmful effect | on

8 bring about | a change

9 will result in | their /
will result in | them

10 had been | ripped off.

11 apologised for | having

12 whether or not | they had

13 was | in the wrong

14 not to | put up with

15 visit took her | by / visit caught her | by

16 matter of time | until/before Thomas
makes/reaches/takes

17 are presented | in a seamlessly

18 more | environmentally friendly

19 as long as | you come

20 take a toll | on

21 needn't | have

22 was unable to conceal | how

23 know (anything about) | how books

24 would be ashamed | of

25 wrong in thinking | highly of

26 at risk | of/from suffering

27 caught a glimpse | of

28 kept him | in the dark

29 even though | the meeting had

30 time will tell | whether or

31 was finally | put off

32 it is impossible | to hide his anger

33 be able to | do without

34 to | make ends meet

35 me know about | the party in

36 have no effect | on the way/how

37 in accordance with | all

38 put/set | the record straight

39 took to | handball

40 (a little) under | the weather

Key

41 must have | failed to

42 rule out | at least

43 is the person | to whom

44 was | called off

45 is no point (in) | trying /
   isn't any point (in) | trying

46 takes pride | in

47 am not | in the mood /
   am | in no mood

48 to come across | as

49 I came | to the conclusion (that)

50 have I | come across (with)

51 taken to find | a solution to

52 are expressing | (their) worries/
   concerns with/in

53 on the/by bus | free of charge/without
   charge

54 was | extremely thankful/grateful

55 not find it easy | to put

56 being | out of order/service

57 came as | no surprise

58 nearly as/so much money | as what

59 was pulled down | after she passed

60 really disappointing | in comparison to/
   with

61 having | no experience in

62 willing to put my life | at

63 advised him | against

64 do not appeal | to me in

65 as to | get rid

66 against the law | to get

67 not find it difficult | to play /
   not find difficulty | in playing

68 don't think very highly | of

69 about what happened, | the more
   confused

70 to avoid | going for/having

71 was/is really fed up | with

72 chat women | up /
   chat | up women

73 have | the slightest interest

74 is no need | for

75 me a call | upon (your) arrival

76 no intention | of getting

77 in hot/deep water | unless

78 are bound to succeed | in /
   are bound to be successful | at

79 can't/couldn't | have been John

80 little likelihood of | him/his

Key

81 making fun/having made fun | of

82 can't/cannot | put me up

83 not to carry on | smoking /
he wouldn't carry on | smoking

84 hitting the books | soon

85 my next job presents/has | fewer
challenges

86 successful at | raising (enough)
successful (enough) at | raising

87 have I met | anyone as/so

88 resulted in | all the crops (being)

89 making | eye contact with

90 didn't get | out of hand

91 regretted not | having brought /
regretted not | bringing the

92 not being able | to afford

93 make any difference | to me

94 all night | long

95 lot keener | on Italian

96 you not | been carrying an antidote

97 are what matters most | to /
are what really matters | to

98 handed in | his notice

99 aware (that) he had | no intention

100 not expected this beer | to be

Made in the USA
Las Vegas, NV
19 March 2024

87419620R10024